Cures for Hysteria

For Karen—
How wonderful to meet—
you. I'm so grateful
you will read my book!
MaryAnn

poems by

MaryAnn L. Miller

Finishing Line Press
Georgetown, Kentucky

Cures for Hysteria

Publisher: Leah Maines

Editor: Christen Kincaid

Cover Art: World History Archive / Alamy Stock Photo. Votive relief, marble.
Found near the Enneakrounon fountain, Athens. From the sanctuary of the
hero-physician Amynon.

Author Photo: Ink Shop, Ithaca, NY courtesy the author.

Cover Design: Elizabeth Maines McCleavy

Printed in the USA on acid-free paper.
Order online: www.finishinglinepress.com
          also available on amazon.com

Author inquiries and mail orders:
Finishing Line Press
P. O. Box 1626
Georgetown, Kentucky 40324
U. S. A.

Table of Contents

Sieves 1

Onset Age Three 5
4AM Ambush...6
The Waiting Room 7
St. Michael's 8
Louie Louie..10
Time Management 11
It Happens Again...12
Smelling Salts 13
I Think I Can Hide 14
State of Grace 16

1956 Diagnostic Exam
Yellow Clinic Children's Hospital Pittsburgh....................................19
Villa Clara...21
La Belle Indifference 22
Galen's Ancient Greek Exam...23
Interpretation of Dreams..24

Dr. Schell...27
Melampus 29
Cures for Hysteria 30
Odor of Linseed Oil 32
Emma Eckstein's Nose 33
Help Me Jesus 34
Dr. Katcher 35
Talk About Guilt..36
Neurological Institute Columbia Presbyterian 37
Capsule...38

Why I Chose to Do the Work 41
Involuntary Recumbency..42
The Idea That Woke Me..43
Far Out on the Comet's Tail 44

Disquisitional...47
Ghazala 52

How Mary Barnes Worked the System..53
Charcot's Iconogrphy 54
Diagnosis by Law Enforcement in Philadelphia 55
Reparative Therapy in California 56
Lunch at the Russian Tearoom 57
Dancing for Maya..58
What it Seems 59
The Misdiagnosis of Ingrid Gamstorp...60
At the Terminus...62

Acknowledgements
Notes

To my children, Camela and Joe,
you have always been my teachers.

You know, MaryAnn, some wags think
women are hysterical, constipated bipeds.

Dr. James Hammill
Neurological Institute
1971

Sieves

This is her last secret,
final dish on the table,
her favorite tastes, what is left.

Forced through a fine sieve wet parts
reassemble on the other side. She is a screen print.
Sitting wrong causes the cells to slip.

There is the sound of lithic chipping, of husks
silent around what form remains.
Remains of mother, sister, cousin, daughter

all forced through sieves hanging beside her.
The sound of shaken grain falling through frame drums
struck for birth, fertility, stolen by military, banned by church.

Her church was a sieve she ran from;
she became her own icon trimmed with gold leaf.
She hung her marriage sieve alongside

her pushed-through parts. The slipped cells
slide away to bloom like printer's ink on a wet page,
an unsigned proof, an edition of one.

*When I say woman, I mean a sex so fragile, so variable, so mutable,
so inconstant and imperfect, that Nature (Speaking in all honor and reverence)
seems to me to have strayed from that good sense by which she had created
and formed all things, when she built woman.*

Hippocrates
c 460–377 BC

Onset Age Three

i.
Presque Isle, Erie, Pennsylvania: beach sun red air.
I am pressed into sand. A trap has sprung.
Her face looms.
Do you have pins and needles?
She drags me up, hands digging into armpits,
my head flops.
She rubs my legs.
Are your legs asleep?
Not just legs, all of me.
Lids stay open when I look down,
eyes ready to pop.

ii.
How paralyzed will I be today? How long will it last?
Maybe I got polio from running around the yard one day in my underpants.
Get in here you'll get infantile paralysis!
My head is filled with ammonia.
Soggy face mashed into the pillow,
I'm nailed to the bed. I can move only fingers and eyelids.
I'm going to suffocate. I strain against
this thing that binds me again and again.
What if it never goes away?
Move or die! Move or die! I labor back to mobility.
From the ceiling, I watch myself writhe,
expect my heart to stop, until I learn it probably won't.
I don't want to die like this.
What if the Russians drop the bomb?
How can I duck and cover?

4 AM Ambush

stomach rebels
metallic odor builds
skin vibrates
muscles become blubber
I'm welded to the bed
legs and arms flatten like a shirt in a mangle
teeth clamp eyelids lag
heart slams in my ears
lungs sucking cotton wad
can't get away

can't get up to pee
hot wet then cold
stink until morning
try to move anything
try to roll, bring a knee up
imagine someone big and fat on top of you
flesh sticking like hot plastic

it passes
I think it's me making it go
that I can work it away
force my muscles into contraction

birdsong at dawn
slows my heart
to sleep

The Waiting Room

smells like babies.
Little sister and I play with creased cloth books,
wooden alphabet blocks;
together in the seat
of a blue hobbyhorse
we rock.

Nurse lays me in the baby scale
curved metal sling, a round dial,
hand to point out pounds, like the grain scale
at Ferguson's General Store.

She rubs my index finger with alcohol,
pierces it with a needle,
a drop of blood onto a glass rectangle.
Doctor listens to my heart,
hits my knees with his red rubber hammer:
Heart murmur and anemia.

To the drug store for a tonic,
butcher shop for marrow bones.
The tonic clear as water
wrinkles my tongue.
Be a good little soldier, Dad says.

St. Michael's

i.
I hide Veronica in my desk
at the back of the fifth-grade class,
dress her for dates with Archie.
Handmade paper doll in a red bathing suit,
wardrobe of pedal pushers, flared skirts,
blouses with stand-up collars.
I've never seen a woman in her underwear,
the proportions are off.
Her bosom is huge.

Sister Leonard swoops at Veronica,
tears the sinful cut-outs into the waste basket.

> (She picks them out of the can.
> I'm so sorry. She arranges them on my desk.
> The pieces reunite—a miracle.)

ii.
Everyone is down the fire escape
practicing safety, but my legs are paralyzed.

Sister stays behind: *What if
there were a real fire?
Someone would have to carry me.*

> (She throws me over her shoulder
> bumping my head on the doorway.
> Everyone cheers as she clatters down
> the fire escape, my arms dangling.)

I claim I don't need confession when the class is herded
down the hill to church for Friday absolution.
I sit in the pew praying. Everyone else
takes their turns in the box with Father Marinaro

(Sister asks me to pray for her sins, to ask
God to give her a special blessing. She
places my hand on her cheek. Tears shine
in her small eyes.)

At ten-thirty children's Mass, Sister Leonard notes
who is not singing the Latin prayers.
Don't chew the host, a girl did that once and choked on the blood.
By communion time I'm glued to the pew.
I don't go to communion.

(I extend my arms out in front,
        fly around the nave.
People duck to avoid my swooping.
They smile as I glide by.
I hover to take communion,
 float back to my seat
wrapped in gold and incense.)

Louie Louie

The purple masked Phantom makes himself flat, slips under the door and is under my bed waiting. I scoot out of bed to the hall. My pin curls are too tight and hurt my head. I feel for the tie on top of my head and loosen the bow. I stand in the doorway of my parents' room silhouetted by the hall light. I softly call, *Mum, Mum, Mum, Mum.* My mother turns over, sits up, screams at my father, *Louie, Louie! It's the Devil!* Where? Where? I look all around. I jump shrieking onto my mother. *Get off! Get off! Dio mio! I thought you were the Devil with those horns sticking out of your head.* She lays me down beside her to sleep. *Settle down. You nearly gave me a heart attack.* I sniff every three seconds. *Stop sniffling. Pazienza di Job!* After a few more sniffs, she leads me back to my own bed and closes the door. A sliver of light shows along the bottom edge. I never tell her about the Phantom. I think about making myself very flat.

Time Management

Summer forays must be timed to slide
between episodes.
I learn to run wild
when I can.

Baseball in the empty lot—it's coming on.
I can't run
but I think I can swing the bat.
They know my legs get weak,
someone is my runner,
but when the ball hurtles at me
all I can do is lift my left hand to stop it.
Shoulder wrenched from the impact,
I limp up the hill home to wait.

Once, on horseback my legs begin to go,
I lose my stirrups, turn back to the barn,
slide off. The girl groom unsaddles for me,
curries my horse, while I seize up
on the wooden bench.
Won't be able to ride my bike back home.

By the time my sister and cousin ride in
I can move around. I lean on my bike,
takes me an hour walking along the highway,
limp for days from the effort.

Soon the penetrating hormones of puberty,
paralysis long and hard.
Standing in the kitchen
blackness takes me.
I return with vertigo-splashed light.
I don't know where I've been.

It Happens Again

when I go out to feed the dog.
I whirl with nothing to hold onto.

       I break: white specks in a black sky,
       Sputnik in the summer night.

I'm splayed on the roof,
fingernails scraping shingles.

       Dog is a jagged zebra,
       fleas on my white socks.

A chain rattles,
binds my ankles.

       Does the dog knock me down?
       Do I collapse?

Smelling Salts

Thinking I fainted
the usher cracks an ampule
under my nose.

If my uterus is
anywhere in the vicinity
it will descend.

I can't move
but am vigilant
in vapors.

I Think I Can Hide

"It's like trying to move someone else's leg with your mind."

—Sarah Manguso

i.
I think I can hide my condition in that
behemoth brick high school,
but, first day, sweet-faced Fawna Lee:
Didn't you have something wrong with your legs?
(Interrupted first communion practice, Sister Grace scowling.)

I grew out of that, I lie.

ii.
Scan schedule, see where I can fall,
when to go upstairs to the girl's room,
walk the block-long building end to end
        safe for PE first period
            art second period, still moving with warning
                third: chemical odor paralysis
                    fourth: working out of it

Flex flaccid muscles during class, trying them out.
Must look like a Tourette's with all that ticking.

By the end of the period, I push myself upright, wait.
Nudge my books around on the desk
until I can pick them up,
        sort of swing the right leg ahead
          hope the left will support me.

Overcoming the inertia of my weight
my calves get really pumped.
Some success, just dear God,
no stairs yet. Clutching books
with left arm, grasping handrail
with right hand, pull my weight up.
Get my right foot onto the step, the left foot

maybe comes along.
Try to get a leg up without
lifting my thighs with my hands or
wait for the halls to clear to have the stairs to myself.
Some days my jaw locks shut, I work a finger
between my teeth to chew. Lunch my savior.

State of Grace

Church was hell—fasting and forced sitting,
all too much for me—give up to the unyielding bench.
Convinced I am epileptic,
I pierce my parents' state of grace.

My father grabs me. *What's the matter with you?*
—*Take me out!*
Encloses me in his arms,
maneuvers me out of the pew,
drags me legs buckled.
Mother follows,
opens the car door.
Dad lowers me onto the back seat.
Head and arms flopping,
I roll into the foot well.
Take me to a doctor. I can't stand this anymore!
Mum says: *I didn't know you were still having that.*

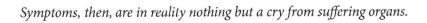

Symptoms, then, are in reality nothing but a cry from suffering organs.

Jean Martin Charcot (1825–1893)

1956 Diagnostic Exam
Yellow Clinic Children's Hospital Pittsburgh

where the poor people go
rows of antiseptic chairs bolted to asphalt tile floor
window above a Formica counter like the post office
my father tells the woman he earns eighty-six dollars
(a month? a week?)
Are we poor?
or lying to get free doctors?

Do you want your mother in the room when I examine you?
No.
He hits my knees with his triangular rubber hammer,
pricks the skin of each arm and leg.
He lifts the cotton gown and becomes
the first person to touch my breasts.
Do you like Elvis Presley? he asks.
I think he's a good singer, but I like Harry Belafonte better.

He writes something on his pad.
When was the last time you felt this weakness?
I'm feeling a little bit of it now.
Where?
I don't like to say (Catholic girl modesty.)
You can tell me, I'm a doctor.
In my bottom.
Not in your toes or fingers?
No.
I don't want him to see me paralyzed.
Get dressed and go to the waiting room.
My mother comes back in, watches me dress.
What did he do?
Nothing. Just checked my reflexes and pricked me with pins.

My legs stiffen.
The clinic smells like ammonia.
Dad helps me to the car.

A letter comes to Dr. Griffin
calling my condition out, revealing
my neurosis. *Exaggerated guilt conversion. Hysteria.*
Psychosomatic.

Do you want to end up in a sanitorium? my mother asks.

Villa Clara, Cagliari Hospital, Sardinia, Italy
Giovanna M. 1823–1913

What scrapes the inside of her ten-year-old skull?
She says it's a "cranky head."
Maybe it's simple *malocchio,*
result of envy, easily treated,
an oily cross traced on her forehead,
mutterings by a wise *nonna.*

1836:
Giovanna migrates south to the basement
of the *manicomo* (madhouse)
avere i nervi (she has nerves)
eccentricico
The only place on the island where the mad, the maniacs
were locked up…50 people in chains,
in the smell of our own excrement, with rats gnawing at our ulcers.

Professor Sanna Salaris
discerns hysteria.
Bathing, tonics, tinctures, polenta poultices,
novel concoctions from chemists of the day,
regular purgings.

Chaos rages outside the walls.
What does Giovanna know?
Mazzini?
Red shirts?
Victor Emmanuel?
My grandparents sail from Salerno to New York.

…eighty years in psychiatric hospital for a headache.

Giovanna, in the cellar
behind the gate,
a cancelled life.

La Belle Indifference

Am I not troubled by my paralysis?
Do I parade it for financial gain
or medical attention like a hospital hobo?
Secrecy is never indifference.
A weak chick could be thrown
from the nest pecked to death.

A peregrinating patient with factitious disorder
would romp from doctor to doctor.
I am not a hospital hopper.
My serene exterior is not indifference
but calm. Trained in tranquility,
I avoid the incipient slap.

Snap out of it!

Because I wear the tin-can corset with two holes punched
in the bottom for my legs,
I know where *la belle indifference* resides.
It's in those who won't believe a female,
not even one they love.

Galen's Ancient Greek Exam

Galen lays hands upon her neck,
virgin chest,
her canny pubis.

He imagines a womb so elastic and pushy
it elbows past kidneys bowel gut,
suffocates the slender throat.

Wandering womb,
rubbery, fecund, the source
of vague complaints inseparable from gender.

The womb is secretive,
prone to slinking. The penis
can be trusted to stay put in plain sight.

Galen makes his best scientific guesses,
treats the invisible other,
woos the empty vessel with chemical sweets.

Interpretation of Dreams

I run
Bare feet brush the grassy ground
I run until the bright horizon swallows my legs

I run on into eternity
never tiring
no body between desire and flight

...we may deduce the doctrine that anxiety dreams
are dreams of sexual content, and that the libido
appertaining to this content has been transformed into anxiety.
Sigmund Freud
The Interpretation of Dreams

Dr. Schell
Psychology Professor, Edinboro University of PA, 1961

Above or below the waist?
Do you mean the paralysis
or someone touching me?
Touching.

Do you have a
boyfriend?
Yes.
What's his name?
J------.
Oh, I know him.
Older than you.

But what about my hysteria?
What can I do to get better?

Your name is Italian.
Yes. My whole family is Italian.
Well,
you may be like a finely bred poodle.
Centuries of breeding within the same
species can produce highly
sensitive nervous systems.

You mean my family is inbred
and that's why I have hysteria?
Could be.
Have you ever taken a tranquilizer?
My doctor at home gave me Librium.

Did it help?
Well, I still get paralyzed but
it makes me feel less upset about it. I don't
take it anymore. I need to get over this.
It's psychological, there should be a
psychological cure, shouldn't there?

Well, it's kind of up to you
if you're going to stop
the guilt feelings that can cause it.

But I don't know what I'm guilty of.

It has something to do with sex.
But I've never had sex.
You're Catholic, right?
So you could feel guilty
even about French kissing.

When I was three years old?
We don't know or can't
remember what happened
when we were that young.

I'm a virgin. Dr. Griffin
told my mother.
Besides I think I'd remember
having sex when I was three.

Come back next week
and we can talk about it some more.

Melampus

Yoked like oxen
the daughters of the King plan a row.
They are mad cows stamping in the meadow.

Heads thrown they refuse to worship the phallus.
Melampus, friend to snakes, calls out their virginity,
their foul humors, sad empty wombs.

He charms them with hellebore.
Why they drink is a mystery.
Purged and flaccid, their vitality sapped,

they are dragged to Dionysis,
initiated into the pleasures of penis and plow,
what they had been missing.

Melampus is rewarded for his great wisdom.
Even now he is considered (by some)
the father of psychiatry.

Cures for Hysteria

induce the uterus to migrate back to its correct place
hold something foul-smelling at the patient's nose
something sweet-smelling at the patient's vagina
the uterus will respond
take care not to coax the uterus below the genitals

remove the erectile turbinate bone from the nose
don't leave any packing gauze behind

apply pressure to the woman's head with your hands
don't release her until she reveals the secret
hypnotize her to relieve the forgotten memory
to talk about dreams and fantasies of her father

effect hysterical paroxysm by stimulation of her genitals
invent a machine to do it as your hand will tire

advise her to refrain from over-excitement
from reading stories
going to the theater or speaking loudly
no intercourse or masturbation
avoid exercise and mood swings

jambul juice mixed with saltwater kept in the sun for a week
drink a cup every day for two weeks
rauwolfia ground into a cup of milk morning and evening
an emulsion of asafoetida by mouth
if the patient resists shoot it up her ass

one teaspoon of honey everyday
macerate bottle gourd place the pulp on the patient's head
one teaspoon of Indian gooseberry juice
to one cup of fresh lettuce give it to patient
every day for a month in the morning

eat only fruit for a month
drink only milk for a month

no tea coffee alcohol white sugar white flour caffeine
teach the patient self-control right habits of thinking
and how to masturbate

relieve stress and regulate body functions
with regular gentle exercise yoga tai chi Pilates
walking swimming massage acupuncture

don't take expensive medications
express yourself to a partner or friend

get away from home
eat more
stop faking
eat dates
jog

stay out of trouble
don't be an inconvenience
don't let your nipples show
don't infect anyone
have an operation on your ankles

read Freud
interpret your dreams
learn auto-suggestion
get hypnotized
remember what happened
stop feeling guilty
get married
have children
act normal

Odor of Linseed Oil

My father gave me a pistol
when I moved to New Jersey.
I pointed it at my face one night,
then gave it back to him.
Set up my easel in the living room.

Emma Eckstein's Nose

Repulsed by the odor in my nose I sit stoic
as Rosanes pulls out a length of pus-soaked gauze
left by Fleiss when he excised
the graceful spiral, my turbinate bone,
heart of my mucosa arousals.

I am brave. I don't make a sound.

Hemorrhage.
I am brave in blood. I do not lay blame.
Freud runs for his cognac.
So this is the strong sex.

But they blame me
for continuing to bleed
for myeloma, my womb finally gone.
I am brave. I keep my nose clean.

Help Me Jesus

Floundering, I turn to Christ,
stop making fun of the Saved,
pray for my own salvation.
Folk mass, Handel's *Messiah*, youth group
spaghetti suppers retreats sleepovers in the church.
Volunteer at the NJ Hospital for Chest Diseases,
take my three-year-old son to visit the elderly, to Head Start,
a model child for the disadvantaged.
He falls out of his chair during Good News Club.
He can't move.
I am bludgeoned by recognition.

I speak at the World Day of Prayer—how Jesus
revealed the cause of my illness through my son.

Father Morris gives the benediction: *May you all
take away the truth of what was said today.*

—as if only part of what I said was truth

An oblique message sent and received,
a splinter in the finger
of logic stinging me awake.

Dr. Katcher

First responder to my disaster,
first to tell me what it really was and how to fix it.
Of all the ways I could have found out, this was
the worst—passing it on
to my three-year-old son.

Dr. Katcher,
handle-bar moustache,
quiet voice, pointing
to people like us in his book.
The truth shall set you free, but it is not for the faint hearted.
And the marriage? No answer for this question until years later.

His compassion edged with excitement, he calls it in
to the station house at Columbia Presbyterian:
"potassium glide" "affected gait."
Later during the genetic panel my son says,
I'm glad Dr. Katcher is a smiling doctor.

Talk About Guilt

No more
pregnancies,
tubal ligation
requires permission from

                                        four men on a hospital panel.

Husband chooses vasectomy,
for one painful day he waddles,

                                      no one utters divorce or death.

Medication withheld from my son,
a year of Bert and Ernie,
consolation from Mr. Rogers,
he would never go down the drain.

How much proof did the lab need?
He repeats nursery school,

                    *

Champion Little League hurler
muscle receptors firing,
cleats, dusty mitt on the floor,
he falls worn out just inside the front door.

At sixteen he topples on stage,
set up like a cardboard Keith by his drummer,
knees locked, guitar braced,
fingers still moveable.
Father's hopes
for a scholarship unravel.

                             It's not your fault, Mom.

Neurological Institute Columbia Presbyterian

.

Back turned,
robe hiked above my hypertrophied calves,
I expose the battle-won swellings of muscle,
in a new language for those fresh residents
who might someday meet a rare bird
like me.

Dr. Hammill: *Tell them.*
And I do, starring in my own unbent narrative
titled by Gamstorp,
funded by Jerry Lewis,
no longer ghost written by Freud.

No twisted postures, no converted emotions,
no fantasy of someone in the night.
Script in this theater written by electromyography,
Muscle and nerve biopsies,

i.
Ten days in this *Salpetriere* teach me the continuum of disorder:
    Patients parade their impaired gaits.
        Catholic nun with twin tumors, each a caduceus
            twisted around arteries in her neck;
                the woman in a white turban of bandages
                who screams all day,

the stagger-step Parkinson's man full of literature and cat stories;
    the schizophrenic lesbian poet who lanks into my room
        just before lights out looking for hurried love as she waits for a bed
        in the psych unit across the street.

She names the tall man with directions written on his scalp *The Golem.*
    He wanders the ward at night walking in and out of rooms a few steps
        ahead of the orderlies.
            I wedge a chair back under the doorknob to keep from reading
            what is inscribed on his head.

Capsule

Hyperkalemic Periodic Paralysis Familial
often misdiagnosed in females as
Hysterical Guilt Conversion
Responds to acetazolamide.

take one each day
Mutation on Chromosome 17
Sodium channel, voltage-sensitive
Type IV cramps familial

serendipity in the sodium channel

Hyperkalemic Periodic Paralysis
Paramyotonia congenita atypical
Gamstorp Disease

Adynamia Episodica Hereditaria
Acetazolamide-responsive
all I need is a pill.

I am startled at the idea that I may have overlooked some organic affection.

Sigmund Freud
Interpretation of Dreams

Why I Chose to do the Work
(School Counselor: 1982–1997)

because people don't pay attention
because children don't have the language
because doctors don't listen
because of the power of psychiatry
because of centuries of medical bias against females
because children kill themselves
because there was no one to listen to their secrets
because illness is often attributed to morality
because religion doesn't help
because schools are where children live

because parents are terrified of blame
because there are experts who need finding
because there are connections to make

between an emotionally incontinent second grade boy and lead poisoning
between a seventh grader with a miscarriage and the school nurse
between a fugitive kindergartner and a pediatric neurologist
between a bully and his Vietnam vet father
between a step-daughter's essay and the prosecutor's office
between the island of silence and the bridge of speech

Involuntary Recumbency

i.
Driving to the new Barnes my muscles seize.
Like the traffic around me on I-95 I am stuck,
right foot spared, in motion from gas to brake,
the ghost in the machine, the silent center
quietly cursing.

ii.
Myotonic goats make good pets
because their fences need only six inches.
Clap your hands to surprise them,
they will seize and slam the ground
in a spontaneous episode.
Dan Rather found them entertaining.
Lucia Perillo says *they teach us to rise.*

iii.
On I-78 returning from
a crisis intervention conference,
my foot freezes to the pedal,
torso slumps. Eighteen-wheeler
behind me, I lift my right leg with both hands,
brake, gliding off to the exit ramp.

vi.
Limping past the reflecting pool
I find Courbet's "Woman with White Stockings."
She leans back to roll the stocking onto her right foot,
her left leg already covered, gartered,
shod in a red slipper,
graceful sole bracing the ground.
Dark dimple of a vagina
between pale fruit buttocks,
hint of inside revealed.
Her eyes hold kind recognition.
She will rise,
continue dressing.

The Idea That Woke Me

They have all left me, I cry at midnight
after a dream of three friends
leaving their horses at the stable,
going on without me, no sign of them
on the rocky mud road.
My cell phone disintegrated,
SIM card crunched in the rutted dirt.
Were they my children?

Motherhood was an infection,
the missing idea
burning at the edges,
soft pillow hiding
a stone wrapped in thin cotton.
It's the awful thing I did that I can't remember.
Thinking of Medea
I bury the dread of being found out.

Far Out on the Comet's Tail
(After Tomas Transtromer)

Far out on the comet's tail where light becomes memory
there is an unmooring,
a possibility of meeting oneself in an exchange of energy.

An expert on NPR shatters the cold of this January
with his theory of recollection.
What we thought we were made of is singed, warped, sifted.

Our airship beats away with no destination,
pulses with a Bolero *ostinato*
or fades into a walk across the street.

Near the end we stand on wobbling particles.
Ahead, we see: unremembered infancies.
Here there is no denial of earthly change.

On the far end we cast lures into a Bethesda pool
gathering mercy and disgrace.
Remember how your spine folded halfway through the journey.

Remember how it felt when everything fell away, how proud you were
buying rugs for your mother
when your bones could take the weight.

We get smaller as we speed up, even as we tarry, we hope
someone is watching
for our return, but we don't care what they think.

When my grandfather died I touched his wooden fingers
and knew he would no longer
shake out an insistent rhythm.

As we head toward the sun it's not so hard to imagine
the knots in our knuckles
splintering into wispy white birds.

"...hysteria in the male is not as rare as is thought," and Charcot's "polyclinics" were filled with hysterical men...This was Charcot's great act of "courage," his "discovery" of masculine hysteria.

Georges Didi-Huberman
The Invention of Hysteria

Disquisitional
(After Daniel Paul Schreber, 1842–1911)

ying in bed I locate bone

        thorns in my amygdala

oft organs muscles tendons melt

        calcifications hold

ong-term potentiation

        kopfhalter belts me in the bed

hinking of Daniel Schreber

        as woman, as Wandering Jew

Translating his nerve-language
ips me into craziness.
 hold my stomach close to the spine
o keep myself straight.

hadowed ossicles like an x-ray

        luminary skull

cromium silhouette

        chalklines of ulna and carpals

ye terrarium growing in the finch feeder

        seeds planted while no one watched

weeping my memory

        will make me busy

while the soft parts wrinkle and rot

eft to rot! Schreber bellowed against it
n vain or out of vanity
iis body saturated, pocket picked.
 check my bank balance to come back to earth
fter floating on a ray of *whore-sun*

fter forty-five years I am saturated

        anti-episodic residing in every cell

geradehalter for neurons

          wayward on rays of potassium

wiggling out through kidneys

          ulcerated ureters

I long for a neat garden hut

          embraced by rows of pea vines

wandering on trellises painted white

Schreber earned days away from the asylum
days with his wife who fed him chloral hydrate,
signed him away, then, herself stroked to death.
A line drawn from Keats running through
Schreber's force tube snaking
in, then out of the Saltpetriere along
the Atlantic cable into stacks of books
by *der psychiaterin* who knew the gaze
of Jews and women.

ii.
at dusk the woman wrings out a grey rag:
words pour into her bucket, pinging like crystal
books in her hut listen for echoes of themselves
intimate as strangers who have been in her bed
no "I" for a woman in *The Red Book* unless she
counts Jung's *anima* telling him *it's art*
only a woman's voice could express such milky
trips into a Schreber-like world,
envy of the unimaginative,
close enough to generate visions
Jung rides a seaside train to his mother's birthday party
harried by flood dreams of yellow water
soaked in mescaline dinging like heavy metal
mercury in Keats's veins

iii.
her writing house
ein schreibestube painted cerulean

yellow shutter
with chartreuse trim
around one wide window
fuschia hanging from eaves
sweet peas train bonewhite

Summerhouse for twilight
in the company of gardeners
the writer leaves her
chaos behind.

A plot of earth found
in a foreign place free of spite
and callow rumor

stillness full and fecund
pekoe tea with bread and butter
staring long into the leaves

seeking prophecy
in an amber cloud
de-hoaxed from
priest's wine ruled
with commanded sin

how could they know
what she writes or needs
to stay even
their histories kept them out
of these small homes
closed against muttering

iv.
the din of science clangs without anyone looking
            sunspots flung down the stratosphere like
                        tantrum children—
woodpeckers drill the eaves of my hut

seeking bee larvae laid by the queen
magma streams DNA from Vesuvius

parenting has become institutionalized
but sometimes an embryo slides down the uterine wall

plants itself in the wrong place and everything changes
Schreber's wife lost five *in utero*
miscarried maybe aborted

His mind was incorrigible
could not be disciplined
into science religion or art

clinging to his evolving female genitalia
he carved an explanatory gender into the body
his father tried to temper with contraptions

made of leather and wood
straps in the blood were more effective

another morning I switch from bones to veins and arteries

dyed red and blue in specimen cats

v.
In my *schriebestube* I'm hiding a Jew.
He showed up one day when my back was bent.
Standing in my chartreuse doorway,
he commanded: *hide me in your body.*
I said, *take off your glasses, they will reflect
your presence and give us both away.*
He fit himself into me head first.
I pulsed to take him in until he was completely
hidden, only a toe left to the cool air.
It didn't keep me from walking,

trying on his glasses.
True proportions became visible,
my right arm swelled with the history of its labors,
voices mumbling in the next sheds magnified.
Neighbors emerged with mattocks,
curses for me naked with a foreign man's toe
instead of a vagina.
I cast the spectacles away.
All was righted but the memory
of my Jew's world.
I have to keep him hidden no matter
how he sobs I suffocate him.

vi.
Let me out and I will tell you stories.
This I can't resist. I pull at his toe.
Briny water seeps as he emerges
taller than I remembered. His black
nerves have risen to his skin giving him
an Ethiopian look. Mapped on his flesh
are branches, menorahs printed from my blood.
I bathe him with rainwater from my copper sprinkling can.
There is a slight salt taste to his shoulder.
I have been many places. Point to a place
on me and I will tell the story of life and death there.

Ghazala

history recorded on cloud day and night
flying through it we discover arrogance

light wanes through a garnet glass
held to the window

there are books unbroken on the shelf
written by mistaken women

I place my hand on the trunk to sense
the weight of the wind

Leonids spray a bright dust
perforating the eastern dark

the soil in that corner needs amending
now that sunlight reaches it

in an apartment in Benevento
we found our house on Google Earth

what happened to you? he asked pointing
to the scars on my shoulders

religion scrapes up meaning but
there are more things in heaven and earth

a fir fell in the night missing
the bed by four standard cubits

a Pashto is sung on the sidewalk
a kite floats to the sand

How Mary Barnes Worked the System

Mary learned to smear her shit just so on the walls
her breasts were shit   her womanhood shit

Imagine a man drawing penises with his own feces
Could he ever devalue his magic like that?

                  Laing paid attention,

he was the one she wanted.
Canny about her place and eager for experience,
Mary pressed on in her *successful schizophrenic voyage*
from regression to liberation.
Mary studied her patients
for sickness and acceptance,
warmed her desire for
volitional madness.

                  She became her own Albert Londe,
                  her hand the camera.

                  Berke missed the ambitious
                  woman as he poked
                  the sexualized infant

No head in the oven for her,
she made it into the galleries.

Mary and Laing together worked their way
from Kingsley Hall to Mare Street,

her smears documented in paint
like tormented Klines
with flame-licked crucifixes.

"Christ Triumphant" hanging
on the wall, an exhausted runner
after a victory lap dragging his sacrifice.

Charcot's Iconography

i.

Sit a *malade* in front of a camera and she
will lose her false innocence begin to pose
hoping to please Monsieur with ever more flighty gestures

The camera does not lie These spontaneous symptoms
truer than the woman within cannot be mimed
Over time they enlarge into eternal evidence

Out of the lark mirror fly broken wings
avid visages. Londe's iconographic array invokes
classification A cavorting catbird captures Monsieur's interest
sooner than a sparrow

ii.

Lay a finger on each face feel the aura of madness
shining from the brow the snappish eyes
Levitation pushes your fingertip convincing
you of schemes beneath this Ouija board
But look, here are your mother's cheeks
sister's chin lover's lips

iii.

Off-camera the director leads the dance
he's a mirror in the ballet studio guiling the women into
fanciful steps he wants to see through the lens
of invention

Diagnosis by Law Enforcement in Philadelphia

He thought he had it covered.
The man produced
a training video
for police officers
on diabetic shock but
was detained as suspicious,
headlights on high beam.

To them he was a drunk
screaming for his fruit punch.
They ignored the bracelet,
broke his left wrist,
clubbed his right hand,
cut his neck, raised a bloody bruise
on his forehead,
treated him like my aging father-in-law
picked up staggering with MS in Aliquippa.

Unarmed, pockets turned out,
Daniel Fried was taken to the ground
clutching at the righteous blue twill
slipping from his grasp,
night lit up with chrome badges.

Reparative Therapy in California

learn to dress like a man
                        walk straight to complete your
                        chromosomal correctness

your urge toward men is
a drive to be repaired
                        a non-gay homosexual

I give to you the same instructions
as the others
                        touch yourself in front of my mirror
I'll stand behind you
cuddle with me   in a non-sexual way

it will heal you
these techniques are designed to help
you be who you really are
                        in a safe place

your parents want only
your happiness   want to uncover
childhood wounds   their guilt

my mission is to enable you
                        to be as God intended

Lunch at the Russian Tea Room

Twelve bas-relief phoenixes
painted gold
undulating to the ceiling
paintings hung salon style
retinal red banquettes
like laps of Ukrainian *babushkas.*
Tablecloth warms my knees.

Who poured from these relic
samovars in niches?

Not this cashmere electronic lunch crowd
their accents recalling childhood meals
in Ukrainian neighbor's homes
without telephones.

In the Russian Tea Room
netgearzero is the
wifi password.
One could leave this brisk cocoon
transport to Moldavia or Siberia
Pussy Riot a click or two away.

Imagine the girlish hooligan faces
hidden in hand-knitted *balaclavas*
boot-stomping on linen tables
frozen slogans piled like down
on the bloody carpet.

Here, peasant food is elevated:
borscht, pirozhok, boiled potatoes, vodka.
Potato peelings, war food, come to mind.

Steaming Darjeeling poured over
sour cherries spooned
into elegant cups
a celebration for getting here
safe in our flimsy voyeurism.

Dancing for Maya
(After Sigalet Landau, Israeli
and 3 channel video
by Mona Hatoum)

stress positions
embracing oneself
throughout torment of hours
wishing for wings

                               two women chaining the beach
                               feet placed a meter apart
                               bodies bent from the waist
                               legs pivoting from the hip
                               hands in the sand scooping
                               a trough filling with surf
                               erasing intersections of infinity

there is no magic here
only physics
we can't measure what goes out
in unending cycles
circles of soldiers
plastic toys on a shore

meaning is off canvas
beamed *Night and Day, Day and Night*
raucous swish of tides
can't be prayed away

What It Seems

outside the window the elm
radiant in ochre rain

gamma knife media tags
penetrate our frontal lobes

can't get away from candidates
announcing their announcements

root soup radiates Costa Rica in green season
Alfieri's cook brought empanadas to the atelier

What would it take to get you back here?
a plane ticket and a place to stay

Reginald Farrow invents a microscopic probe
detects electrical signals between cells

Barry Commoner and progressing mutations—
maybe mine, maybe some of that autism

carrots and sweet potatoes are from Whole Foods
an organic insurance policy

Dr. Pacini discovered the cholera bacillus
Dr. Koch took the $40,000 prize for it

Great Chain of Being, a rhizome snaking under soil
where the Hottentot's vagina was buried with her body

I walk out to check for mail
dog next door barks like he's never seen me before.

The Misdiagnosis of Ingrid Gamstorp

In shorts and sandals I separate irises
compacted from the bedding doe
scanning for deer ticks—
better chance to spot the sickening bloodsuckers
on bare legs traveling up to moisture
where I have found them three times,
tweezed them out,
got tested.

Had Ingrid seen the one infecting her,
she would have taken it
to her microscope—
mysterious illness sloughed off for fifteen years
as "woman's complaint."

I pull at the thuggish *clematis autumni*
but it's in a strangle hold around lilac roots.
Sweden's one female pediatric neurologist

named my disease
the same year I was called a hysteric.

Bee-balm, spirea, snap of my shears

adynamia, snip
episodica, snip
hereditaria, snip

Dry spores from ostrich ferns showering my feet.
Fifteen years she was patted on the shoulder
until a friend said Lyme Borreliosis.
Ingrid was damaged beyond repair.
I yank at bindweed, uprooting phlox along with it.
Both of us served sentences
in the prison of disregard.

Maker of doctors who

stole her triumph,
in the end, she was only a woman.
I give up on the coral rose that
hasn't bloomed since Y2K,
cut it to the ground.

At the Terminus

At the terminus a wall becomes a garment
weighing as much as a pound of feathers.

Vitreous projections shooting color under the eyelids
prove a deeper life inside.

The journey will end in an explosion weighing
as much as a pound of iron.

The cormorant's feathers are oily and weigh
more than a pound of sparrows.

A heron's neck becomes an S
signifying spartina and yes.

Wear the wall like a cloak
a friend has wrapped around your shoulders.

Feather it with shadows and light as if
it were a half-opened door.

Within the feathered wall there are mirrors.
Outside they are windows reflecting stunned water birds.

At the terminus a wall becomes skin,
layers of plaster and paint beating.

Stillness settles where the wing meets the joint.
Skin is soft whistle weighing nothing.

Acknowlegements

The courage to persist in writing *Cures for Hysteria* came from friendships and associations with these remarkable people: Ann Kaier, Alison Gold, Carolyn and Kent Kinney, Curlee Raven Holton, David Brigham, David Sterry, David Wojahn, Hila Ratzabi, Holly Trostle Brigham, Jase Clark, J. C. Todd, Joe Stuby, Kasey Jueds, Kathy Sheeder Bonnano, Lee Upton, Liz Abrams-Morley, Michael Northen, Peter Murphy, Sandra Beasley, Shevaun Brannigan, and Vasiliki Katsarou.

I am deeply grateful to all of them and to the publishers who gave the following poems legs.

"At the Terminus" was published in the *Stillwater Review*, Spring 2016

Cures for Hysteria was reviewed as an unpublished manuscript under the title *La Belle Indifference* in Wordgathering, September 2015.

"Why I Chose to Do the Work" and "Far Out on the Comet's Tail" were published in Wordgathering, September 2015.

"Ghazala" was published in the *Musehouse Journal,* Spring 2013, and *Another Breath Anthology*, Rosemont College, December 2014.

"Involuntary Recumbency" and an excerpt from "Neurological Institute Columbia Presbyterian" were published in *Wordgathering,* September 2013.

"Capsule" was published in another form in *Kaleidoscope Magazine*, 2013.

"Louie Louie" was published as a limited edition artist's book through the Experimental Printmaking Institute, Lafayette College, Easton, PA. 2008.

Notes

"Villa Clara": Giovanna M. was sent to the madhouse at age ten and diagnosed with hysteria. She finally died at age 90 in Villa Clara on Sardinia, Italy. *And you'd better believe it: I was 90 years old. Fate, which takes away healthy, free, young people, never pardoned me once. It has let me live all this time, quite lucid, but closed up in here...since I was ten years old*

"*La Belle Indifference*": A naive, inappropriate calmness or lack of concern in the face of one's disability, often seen in those with conversion disorder but no longer considered "pathognomonic" for conversion disorder.

"Ancient Greek Physical Exam": Galen was an Ancient Greek physician who theorized the womb wandered inside a women's body causing maladies referred to as hysteria based on the Greek word for womb (*hustera.*)

"1956 Diagnostic Exam Yellow Clinic Children's Hospital Pittsburgh": The term conversion disorder was first used in1894 by Freud and Breuer to refer to the substitution of a somatic symptom for a repressed idea. This behavior exemplifies the psychological concept of 'primary gain', i.e. psychological anxiety is converted into somatic symptomatology, which lessens anxiety. The 'secondary gain' of such a reaction is the subsequent benefit that a patient may derive from being in the sick role. Criteria for conversion disorder are modified to emphasize the essential importance of the neurological examination, and in recognition that relevant psychological factors may not be demonstrable at the time of diagnosis

"Melampus": Melampus is a figure from Greek history who gained the favor of a king and the "hand" of one of his daughters by curing the daughters of acting like wild cows. Melampus was famous for taming snakes.

"Cures for Hysteria": Some of these cures are ancient, some contemporary. One of the earliest involved holding something with a pleasant aroma at the vagina (as if it could sense) and something unpleasant at the patient's nose. The theory was the womb would naturally descend to the good aroma. Some of these cures were suggested to me by various doctors.

"Emma Eckstein's Nose": Emma Eckstein was a patient of Freud and his physician friend, Fleiss who operated on hysterics' noses to remove the spongy turbinate bones they believed contributed to the sexual arousal of these women. Emma lived through a severe infection, continued to be Freud's patient and eventually became a psychotherapist herself. Her face was disfigured from the surgery and she died in her sixties.

"Neurological Institute Columbia Presbyterian": *Salpetriere* was a hospital in Paris where Dr. Charcot and his disciples paraded hysterics before groups of medical students and others to demonstrate the condition. They were photographed and classified. Freud was a follower of Charcot and visited his arena. Electromyography is a test involving the insertion of needles into muscle tissue to measure the strength and frequency of electrical energy occurring in the muscles.

"Capsule": Hyperkalemic Periodic Paralysis with Myotonia is sometimes misdiagnosed as conversion disorder. Acetazolomide, or Diamox, is a treatment for the episodes of paralysis. It works as a diarrhetic, driving out excess potassium that has built up in muscle cells. The treatment was discovered through research funded via Jerry Lewis for the Muscular Dystrophy Association at the Neurological Institute, NYC. The discovery of acetazolamide as a treatment was "serendipitous" to a search for an anti-episodic for epilepsy.

"Disquisitional": Daniel Paul Schreber (1841-1911) was a German judge who committed himself to an asylum in 1893 at age 51, suffering from delusions and hallucinations. He had been turned down for membership in the Reichstag. He was dosed with chloral hydrate for insomnia. Daniel spiraled into deeper madness but was able to write about his life in the asylum. Both Freud and Jung read his *Memoir of My Nervous Illness*. Daniel's famous father, Moritz, invented several contraptions and systems to keep children disciplined and in correct posture. Moritz is also credited with establishing community garden plots in German cities, each with its own garden hut.

"Ghazala": Ghazala Javed was a Pakistani Pashto singer who was shot to death by gunman hired by her ex-husband as she walked along a city sidewalk.

Other members of her family were also shot. Her ex-husband was sentenced to hang.

"How Mary Barnes Worked the System": Mary Barnes was a nurse who became a psychiatric patient. She was able to mimic the symptoms of her former patients as an avenue to gaining attention for her painting. Her work is still available for purchase through Joseph Berke's website.

"Charcot's Iconography": Jean-Marie Charcot engaged several photographers to record the visages and postures of mad and hysterical patients in his medical theater at the Salpetriere in Paris. Albert Londe was prominent among them. Arrays of photos were composed and used to classify the patients. The patients posed in continually stranger gestures, and so were complicit in creating a system validating hysteria.

"Diagnosis by Law Enforcement in Philadelphia": Daniel Fried produced a video for law enforcement officers on how to deal with diabetics they might stop for traffic violations, perhaps mistaking them for drunks. He was stopped and assaulted by police who hadn't seen it and who ignored his medical bracelet.

"The Misdiagnosis of Ingrid Gamstorp": Ingrid Gamstorp was a Swedish pediatric neurologist who studied in the United States on a grant from the Muscular Dystrophy Association. She named Hyperkalemic Periodic Paralysis: *adanamia episodica hereditaria*. Ironically, she is referred to as "he" in a You-Tube video from the Periodic Paralysis Association 2014 conference.

MaryAnn L.Miller's book of poems *Locus Mentis* was published by PS Books (2012.) Miller holds a BS in Art Education/English, M.Ed. in School Counseling, MFA in Creative Writing (2011) and a Postgraduate semester with the poet David Wojahn at Vermont College of Fine Arts (2012.) She is a Pushcart Prize nominee for 2017. Her poems have been published in *Stillwater Review, Philadelphia Poets, Musehouse Journal, Wordgathering, Kaleidoscope Certain Circuits,* and others. Miller's work is part of the anthologies "Dark as a Hazel Eye" from *Ragged Sky Press* and "Another Breath" *Rathella Press.* Her documentary essay on the printmaking of artist Willie Cole was published in *The International Review of African American Art.* Her video, Haiku Summer 2016, was screened through Scribe Video of Philadelphia. Miller is the designer of the Live Your Dream Award Broadsides sponsored by Rittenhouse Square Soroptimists. She is part of the ekphrastic poetry groups: Chroma and Garden State Hybrids. She publishes hand bound artist books pairing artists and poets through her press: www. luciapress.com.

Miller was the Resident Book Artist at the Experimental Printmaking Institute, Lafayette College since 2001. Miller has held residencies at Vermont Studio Center, Virginia Center for Creative Arts, Universidad Metropolitana Autonomia, Mexico City, University of Costa Rica, and the Ragdale Foundation. Her work has been exhibited internationally. Her artist books are in the National Museum of Women in the Arts, and Special Collections at Bryn Mawr College, William Paterson University, University of Iowa, Herron Art Library, Wesleyan University, Skillman Library, Lafayette College, Smith College, and Stanford University. She has designed and bound a book with the poet Nikky Finney now in the collection of President and Mrs. Obama. Miller is the Poetry Coordinator for the NJ Book Arts Symposium.

CPSIA information can be obtained
at www.ICGtesting.com
Printed in the USA
LVHW091549200220
647643LV00005B/1089

9 781635 344097